I0191319

IS THIS WHY

AFRICA IS?

Copyright © 2014 by Marricke Kofi Gane

IS THIS WHY AFRICA IS?

By Marricke Kofi Gane

ISBN: 978-1-909326-20-0

All rights reserved solely by the author. The author guarantees
all contents are original and do not infringe upon the legal
rights of any other person or work. No part of this book may be
reproduced in any form without the permission of the author.
For permission requests and others, write to the Author at:

author@marrickekofigane.com

Published by MarrickeGanePublishing

Distributed by Amazon·

IS THIS WHY AFRICA IS?

By Marricke Kofi GANE

Contents

DEDICATION

This book is dedicated to the African;

To Africans not by reason of birth or heritage, no;

To those bold enough to believe our Africa can still rise;

To those fearsome enough to believe in Africa's own possibilities;

To those brave enough to demand that Africa gets its share of the world;

To those who faithfully defy the failures that plagued all our fathers' hopes;

To those angry enough to dare see it change for good, even if beyond their time;

To those unafraid enough to venture to ask the hard questions about Africa;

To those willing not only to answer, but also challenge themselves by it;

To those avowed that our children must never ask why we failed;

To those conscientious enough to see it a duty to God;

To those undeterred by obstacles to our change;

Not even by God, by blood, by devils.

I

In The Beginning Was Pride, Then Hope, Then...

I spent a part of my childhood with my grandparents along the coast of the Volta region of Ghana. We lived on a coconut plantation, right in between the ocean and the lagoon. Fresh food and coconut juice I didn't cherish back then, I soon found out growing up, were luxuries and not what I'd wrongly viewed as basics. That's what my modest grandparents told me – that our life was a fairly basic lifestyle and that as long as we had God, food and a little money, that's all we needed. My grandfather would tell me stories about western merchant ships that used to dock off the beach front and how they would bring supplies to the coast in exchange for other things. Life was good by our own standards back then. That was Ghana, part of my childhood.

In Nigeria, another part of my childhood unfolded in the very early 1980s. I was sojourning with my father firstly in Jos, then Kaduna and finally in Makurdi in Benue State. Oh, the thrilling excitement at month ends when my dad would drive me over in his new blue VW Beetle to Emeka's house where we were always guaranteed pepper soup and cow foot. I can still hear the resounding laughter of Mr Nti *(the shortest of the lot)*, my father and perhaps six others, ego-trading over a game of cards or draughts. He was a successful building technologist at a time when Nigeria too was flourishing.

In these memories, I recall the lengthy stories my grandfather used to tell about the pride they had in their time, about Ghana's independence and the grand vision Kwame Nkrumah had to make her, and the rest of Africa, stronger in unity. My father's hope was that the steady but little progress Nigeria and Ghana had chalked up would increase and that someday, Africa too would be viewed collectively as a "first-world" continent. It was the first time I had heard the term "first-world" and each time I asked him which number world we currently were, he would wisely answer, "The most important thing is that if we stay focused, we would also be called that soon." Such were the pride and hopes of my forbearers.

At the time of writing this book, my grandfather has been gone a while now and the pride of grandeur he used to be filled with about what unity could bring to Africa has been shattered, and certainly not from the weight of his coffin. As for my father, who is not known to give up once he has set his mind on something, what he said to me was contrary to his nature. When I last visited him in Ghana, he confided in me: "I have to be honest with you son, living in this country is getting harder and harder by the day." And so too, for many across Africa who are losing hope.

As an international development worker, I have travelled the length and breadth of Africa, and apart from a few countries in the North and a few others dotted around the South, by and large, Africa remains grossly underdeveloped and very much behind the times. It has kept me up on many occasions pondering, long before I mustered the courage to write about it. More interestingly, I have had great difficulty in determining how, if at all, I should define my own hopes and pride for Africa. Yes, at forty, having travelled the world and seen Africa from new perspectives, me and many others have often asked the question: why hasn't Africa progressed much? After the struggles for independence, it would appear as though all we got in return was the curse of a paradox – a sarcastically painful one which took away our oppression and gave us freedom – and with it, war, starvation, greed, corruption, non-development and eroded hopes.

Standing back today, it's easy to see the "life" of Africa as one that never ceases to be oppressed – maybe I am not far wrong in thinking that. Perhaps, we simply traded one refined form of oppression for an outdated version. Physical slavery, we may have exchanged for a mental one; an oppression with guns and ships for one with systems, know-how and our very own mediocrity; ownership through foreign presence for that with local puppets and remote bosses; human slaves for the enslavement of resources that could have transformed slaves to princes; deception by the voice of masters for deception by the voice of Africa's supposed partners and sadly, the greed of her own leaders. Oh, how bitter a man's own gall.

In setting out on this journey, I recognized how few have ever attempted to answer the big question of why Africa has turned out the way that it has. Why has it failed, if indeed it has failed? But, of course, it is wise not to answer such a question because in that question lies Africa's past, present and future, all of which I know not fully. Indeed it is not a weight any one man could carry. My purpose for writing this book is not to answer the questions, but to ask the same questions in other ways, albeit more acceptably. The purpose for writing this book is to hopefully cause some awakening in the minds of my fellow Africans, not by pointing accusing fingers at anyone, but by challenging us all to ponder and brood over the issues.

My approach will be mostly rhetorical with the view that by so doing, it will draw us closer to our personal convictions on how far we've come as Africans, and more importantly, where we ought to be heading in our new dispensation as Africans. This book is not sympathetic to Africa, rather, it is critical of it on many fronts and rightfully so. I do not believe that *I can wake a dying man from sleep by whispering a love song into his ears. No, I must jostle him with a force likened to that of the fierceness of the battle between life and death.*

This work was never intended as a scientifically researched opus, but rather, it is philosophically inclined and honestly presented. It is up to the readers to accept those things which resonate deeply within them and which cannot be ignored because they so merely wish, or to equally reject them, knowing well they will have to contend with their conscience for a long time coming. Either way, our paths will have crossed because of Africa. I have learned that truth ought not be truth merely because one can see, hear, smell, taste and feel the evidence that supports it, or because as a result of these, the mind by virtue of logic, agrees to it as truth. A greater truth is one that the heart concedes to before the mind fathoms it. Indeed it is one which, unlike the mind that holds it, cannot be directed, least of all, controlled.

It is my hope that those who read this book, will one way or another, be met with every truth there is in it, whether or not they have overwhelming evidence to the contrary.

2

Can Someone Please
Tell Me Why?

When Pan-Africanism started I was not yet born and it might be even fairer to say, I don't believe my parents had even remotely considered my conception at the time. That's how far away I was from the concept, let alone the movement. But growing up in a country like Ghana, it can be forgiven if I claimed Pan-Africanism was somewhat detectable in the atmosphere. The late Dr Kwame Nkrumah's sixth of March, 1957, independence speech reiterated the meaninglessness of Ghana's independence except it was linked to the total liberation of Africa. This was infectious in my early years. Its potency was enough for me to have an epiphany of the striving for African oneness. What I couldn't catch from him, I got from listening to Robert Nesta Marley, also of blessed memory.

Typically however, that identity with the philosophy of African oneness raised more questions in my mind than it did answers. At first, I asked just a few, but like a self-mutating mental monster, they soon grew and grew - most of which I could not possibly include in this book for lack of space. Throughout, my focus was never really on finding answers so that I could figuratively go stand in the middle of Africa and unite all her countries. No, I just wanted to know WHY almost everything was seemingly stagnant in Africa's development. Why the widespread mismanagement of so large a wealth of natural resources? Why weren't we making discoveries? Why the famine in highly fertile soils? Why weren't we creating solutions to our own problems? Why the widespread corruption? Why the wars? Why the greed? Why?

Having grown up since, I realise these were not just my questions – they were questions we all as Africans ought to ask. They were questions to inspire our minds to inquire; to make us restless in our thinking; to make us question our own selves and the status quo. They are questions that, hopefully, will liberate us from ourselves – a liberty that I can only hope will someday give me the answers to the "whys" that I ask of anyone reading these thoughts of mine.

I am told that civilisation may have started in ancient Egypt, which very well could be true. After all, with all our modern scientific and technological advancement, the methods and technology used in constructing the pyramids still remain largely inexplicable to our modern day scholars. So, I have genuinely pondered, if civilisation started in ancient Egypt, albeit even remotely, what happened to the rest of Africa? Why didn't she catch up? Can someone please tell me why?

I am told that Africa was once colonised and enslaved. I have often wondered - how is it that a few nations in the world could enslave such a large and vast continent given that some of these colonial nations were much smaller in size than the African countries they enslaved? Was Africa merely a trophy game in the wild, shot and kept by these colonial hunters? Did Africans not fight enough to resist their obvious enslavement? Surely, it couldn't have just been the mesmerizing effects of gunpowder and matchsticks westerners brought ashore, or could it? Can someone please tell me why?

I am told that Africa now has its freedom. Really? So how is it that the rest of the world tells her which economic policies to use, what types of governments to have, how her peoples must relate to each other, how she ought to manage her resources, whether she has the right to defend her people in the manner the rest of the world does and what religious alignment is right or wrong? I wonder; did the rest of the world embrace these approaches in their own democratic development? Why, then, does Africa need to accept them? Why has Africa also believed over time, that its safety does not lie within her but in the redemptive power of others? Can someone please tell me why?

I am told that the continent of Africa has one of, if not, *the richest* concentrations and mix of natural and human resources, vast portions of the former which are still untapped. If Africa chose to, could she live without needing to depend on the world? Could the world live without the resources of Africa? Doesn't she who bakes the bread set the price? So how is it that the resources of Africa are not priced by Africa? How is it that in so many cases the resources of Africa are not even owned by Africa? Why is it that with all her vast deposits of natural resources, Africa still holds out her begging bowl, moulded in gold and begging for quarters, dimes and pennies? Can someone please tell me why?

I am told that the people of Africa are more diseased; more starved and die more than on any other continent. So how is it, that China and India combined, with their vast and unimaginable populations and limited natural resources do not face the same desperate plight as Africa? Did they say "no" to something Africa said "yes" to? Did they say "yes" to something Africa said "no" to? Can someone please tell me why?

I am told that Africa is the most corrupt continent in the world. It made me wonder! Are there not others filthier in their corrupt natures than Africans? On what basis is it determined that Africa is the most corrupt and by whom is it determined? Is it because the corrupt acts of others are hidden from the glare of us all that makes them less corrupt? Could Africa say the same – that others too are equally very corrupt? How about the corrupt acts of those who lie to the world in the name of making it a better place for the global community? How about those who manipulate the news the world hears in order that many may by themselves become the endorsers and justifiers of corrupt agendas? How about the corruption of those who wrongfully enter into other nations to steal away the lives, wealth, hopes and dreams of many in the name of democracy and partnership? Is it because the magnitude of their corrupt acts is above the standards that define corruption? How about the corruption of those who sit in holy righteousness, judging the world on the rotten scales of dubiously sculptured equity? So how is it, that voices other than Africa's are accepted by Africa on how corrupt she is? Can someone please tell me why?

I am told that more aid is needed for Africa. In response I bowed my head in pity and shook it in disgust. Who now gives to Africa, aid on which she may survive? What manner of curse is this, that Africa cannot till her own soil and eat from her own ground? I have, like you, wondered: from where did the saints who now bestow such loving graces of humanitarian and economic aid on Africa gain their wealth? Could it be that the same wealth of ivory, coltan, diamonds, timber, gold, copper, black blood and black sweat taken from Africa by wanton greed in decades gone by and now, have returned under the pitiful cloaks of foreign aid and the exploitive salutations of development partnerships? Why is it that the goose that once laid the golden egg has itself become an egg, needing help to hatch? Can someone please tell me why?

I am told that Africa lacks leadership that has the continent's interest at heart? Really? Isn't that paradoxical? Hasn't Africa produced some of the greatest leaders who stood firm for the philosophy of "united we are stronger"? I wonder why it is that great leaders such as Kwame Nkrumah, Patrice Lumumba, Nelson Mandela, Samora Machel and others of respected and blessed memories got "neutralized" at every juncture they started preaching "African unity." What if these great Pan-Africanists of our times were eliminated? Or perhaps it was just mere coincidence that "some people" did not think it was in their good interest for Africa to become united. I may be wrong, but I may very well be right. Can someone please tell me why?

I am told that armed violence in Africa has denied her opportunities to become a better continent. I have heard many argue that the colonial powers of old are to be blamed for these destabilizations. But wait a minute! How is it that Africa blames her rulers of old? How is it that in spite of Africa's pain, diseases and hunger, she still considers it a priority to kill her own people? Is it not the men of Africa's own womb killing her children? If the tables were turned and if Africa were to put guns and axes in the hands of her colonial rulers, would they slaughter their brothers in the streets in a manner befitting pigs? Would they happily defile their sisters with insane lust? How is it then, that such is the case with the children of Africa? Can someone tell me why?

I am told that Africa should make an effort to learn democracy and good governance from the "*more developed*" countries. And I have often wondered why? Surely, there must have been a time when these "developed" countries were undeveloped, and at the time when they were in this state, did they practice the same "democracy and good governance" that they now beseech Africa to employ? And what exactly defines a developed or underdeveloped nation? Is it the paved roads or the speed with which a nation hurries to reach the end of time, or the proliferation of nature's destruction? Is it the extent to which a nation dilutes its own identity and culture or the profundity of its striving to consolidate power and rule over others? Indeed, I too must ask: is democracy the only way for Africa's evolution? Should it, of necessity, operate in a like manner because it has worked for the developed countries who preach its rightness? Who influenced their evolutions? Why do "they" get to decide, seek to influence, or be the ones to determine the path of evolution Africa must follow? And why does Africa so willingly oblige by refusing to find the governance that works for her? Can someone please tell me why?

I am told that the "*more able nations*" of the world must support Africa in its re-building process. No! Not at all! I do not stand against genuine help, but I am baffled that the same "*able nations*" that supplied the guns and munitions for Africa's wars, now wish to restore Africa to glory. Who gets paid for the supplies of munitions that fuel Africa's wars? And who gets paid for the re-building of Africa? Surely, Africa does not buy its own gold or diamonds or timber or coltan or copper or oil that seemingly forms the basis of its wars. Neither do countries that manufacture arms and munitions do so for the pleasure of erecting them as monuments of bliss. So, I ask, who then has a profitable motive for both the wars and reconstructions in Africa? You tell me, sir; you tell me, madam. From whom are the resources taken to pay for these re-building-cum-development agendas if not from the very people broken by the wars and economic strangulation? So, why and for how long will Africa rape herself to fill the bellies of its predators? Can someone please tell me why?

I am told that in Babylonian times a people became strong and built a tower that reached to the heavens. I am told that even God in heaven acknowledged their oneness of language as a force capable of achieving anything they so wished. I perceive then, that language is a powerful thing – it is like a vehicle by which thought is conveyed from one man to another. Those who speak a language not their own, are like those who wish to convey their wares from home to market but at the mercy of he who owns the vehicle and who decides whether the former's wares are transported or not. Why, then, is it the case that Africa adopts as her own, the languages of foreigners and brutal colonial masters? Is it a well-reasoned ploy that although physical slavery is no more, yet Africa's freedom has no vehicle of expression other than through languages that bind her allegiance to the dreaded kings and queens of the past? If so, why – why are their languages acceptable for adoption and Africa's indigenous aren't? Why is it that if I speak a foreign tongue, I am considered knowledgeable and refined, even though the majority of my own people do not understand me? Can someone please tell me why?

I am told that the history of colonialism still looms large over Africa. Does it? Maybe it is because Africa wants it to be so. No! Maybe it is because Africa is simply lazy and wishes to have something on which to blame its incapacities. I am inclined to believe that history is written to change the future, so I have often asked myself why Africa's colonial history has been blamed for stunting its growth and why has her history of decades past become a justification for retrogressive self-pity? Haven't some of these colonial masters themselves been in wars? Haven't they been colonised one way or another during their evolution? Couldn't they have decided to sit, arms folded, and be underdeveloped by virtue of the same justification of historical oppression? But did they? What then is the justification Africa thinks she has? Why does she think the whole world has an obligation to feel pity for her historical demise? Why won't Africa move on from this mountain of self-absorbed defeatism that it has embraced for so long? Can someone please tell me why?

I am told that uniting Africa is the key to ending her woes. I believe that, although it would not necessarily solve all problems, it would be a useful aspiration. But do the leaders of Africa believe it too? Can someone show me some sign so I too may be convinced they do? Will that unity happen with northern Africa convinced that she is more European than African? Will that unity overcome the barrier of artificial division that sees countries fragmented along English-speaking, Portuguese-speaking and French-speaking lines, all of which are artificial divisions?

Would it happen with the central bloc of Africa, independent, yet serving as the personal garden of the devil's advocates by virtue of her being phenomenally endowed with natural resources? Will that unity be permitted by the greed of Africa's leaders for whom disunity provides the perfect breeding ground for their control and Swiss-siphoning wealth sprees? Why are our economic and development policies only country-specific, with no major regional elements? Why are our regional trades less collaborative and more expensive than those conducted outside Africa? What parts of our educational systems show, that consideration is being given to future African integration? And yet they speak loudly about harnessing the economic potentials across Africa? Why? Why should I believe our leaders when they proclaim that Africa will unite? Can someone please tell me why?

3

Could It Have
Been The Curse?

In the Holy Bible, part of the story of Noah and the great flood is recounted in the book of Genesis, chapter 9. It tells of some interesting occurrences after the great flood as follows:

*"18 Now the sons of Noah who went out of the ark were Shem, Ham, and Japheth. And Ham was the father of Canaan. 19 **These three were the sons of Noah, and from these the whole earth was populated.** 20 And Noah began to be a farmer, and he planted a vineyard. 21 Then he drank of the wine and was drunk, and became uncovered in his tent. 22 And Ham, the father of Canaan, saw the nakedness of his father, and told his two brothers outside. 23 But Shem and Japheth took a garment, laid it on both their shoulders, and went backward and covered the nakedness of their father. Their faces were turned away, and they did not see*

their father's nakedness. 24 So Noah awoke from his wine,
and knew what his younger son had done to him. 25 Then
he said: **"cursed be Canaan; a servant of servants he shall**
be to his brethren." *26 And he said: "blessed be the Lord,*
the God of Shem, and may Canaan be his servant. 27 May
God enlarge Japheth, and may he dwell in the tents of Shem;
and may Canaan be his servant." 28 And Noah lived after
the flood three hundred and fifty years. 29 So all the days
of Noah were nine hundred and fifty years; and he died.
[Genesis 9:18-29, NKJV]

Biblical scholars and historians alike over the centuries have
raised different arguments about where, on today's global map,
these three brothers eventually settled and with them therefore, the blessings or curses they possessed. Varying accounts
have speculated that the three brothers represented Caucasians,
Blacks and Mongolian races. In some anthropological writings,
others have said these three spread out to create the continents
of the earth, in which case the immediate flaw of the argument
arises from the fact that there are three brothers, but five or seven
continents, depending on whose account you choose. Besides
these, other anthropological and biblical historians have further
raised two basic contending arguments amongst themselves.
Firstly, that the phrase *"saw his father's nakedness"* alludes to a
homosexual rape which in itself is a very contentious idea and in
some other schools of biblical thought, it is contended to mean

the raping of Noah's wife *(the latter better explains why Canaan, the son of Ham, instead of Ham, was cursed – being the seed of an evil violation)*. Secondly, there is a controversy over whether or not Ham, or his son Canaan who was cursed by Noah into perpetual servitude, became the father of the black race.

The Bible narrative holds strongly to the fact that Noah had one wife at the time of his boarding the ark. It is therefore logical to deduce that if all three sons came from the same mother, then it was impossible for them to have gone on to become the three different races – Caucasians, Blacks and Mongolians. So, an obvious question to ask would perhaps be: did Noah have his three sons from women other than the wife with whom he boarded the ark? Or, perhaps with the other women aboard the ark who were already referred to as his sons' wives, or with other women who didn't end up officially as his wives and who therefore may have perished in the flood. Alternatively, a final possible permutation of inquiry could be that all the sons of Noah were of the same race, but the son of Ham, Canaan, wasn't – perhaps because his mother was of the black race. Could that have been? Is that the reason why Noah did not curse his own son the perpetrator, Ham, but rather, his grandson, Canaan, who it is suggested, became the final embodiment of the black race? Or was Canaan cursed because the true account *(as asserted by one logical school of thought)*, is that Ham slept with his father's wife *(Leviticus 18:8 – a father's nakedness is his wife),* and in which case Noah saw reason to curse Canaan, the outcome of such an accursed act?

But was Noah's wife of the black race? If not, the big question hangs: *why is Canaan said to be the accursed father of an accursed black race?*

Is that what really happened? Is that single curse of damnation into servitude, the reason why Africa is in her generally stagnated state – always serving or being used to serve the interests of others and never her? Is it the curse of Noah that has bound our very existence as a people and, for that matter, our progress in all respects? I hear many chuckle and scream in their minds, *"Oh, spare me such ludicrous nonsense!"* Indeed I could spare you; but do we know for a fact whether this is an unchangeable truth, a tale of fantasy or a fiction with malicious intent? Or shall we behave like typical human beings, who regard as ludicrous, wild, baseless and insane, anything larger than what their minds can grasp, or that is mentally indigestible for their reasoning abilities – and instead, judge as "real," only those things that their minds can fathom? Is this curse indeed a verifiable truth? Is Canaan's headship of the African lineage a mere fallacy dismissible without justifiable proof? Again, I ask, is Noah's curse, the reason for Africa's lingering chronic problems?

Is this curse of damned servitude, the reason why Africa's intelligent many are unpardonably happy to leave the shores of Africa for faraway countries to serve in degrading jobs, or in most other cases, jobs far below their qualifications? Yet they find every reason other than insanity, to justify such misplaced contentment. Is this the real reason for the brain drain? Is this why Africa will always cultivate excellent minds, only for them to go off and serve in every other nation but their own? Is this curse the reason why Africa's rich mineral and natural resources have never found a way to cure her obnoxious poverty, sickening hunger and disgraceful bouts of malnutrition – but nevertheless, serve the luxurious lifestyles and progressive economic expansion of other countries? Is this curse the reason why foreign income, generated from her consolidated continental labour force, never gets the chance to fully serve her own domestic development but rather the economies of other countries through the re-payment of loan after loan after loan?

Could it really be true? Just peradventure, could it really be that this curse still exists and is the reason for our seeming stagnation?

Is this curse of servitude the reason why like servants, Africa owns nothing of her own? Is this the reason why a greater majority of companies commercially extracting gold, diamonds, coltan, copper and oil out of the lands and waters of Africa are from countries beyond Africa's coastline? Is this the reason why the majority of the technical know-how, machinery and systems we are trying to use in our own development are likely to be the result of the ingenuity of countries outside of Africa? Is this why even our economic and development policies are based on prin-ciples, philosophies, schools of thought, hypotheses, theories and laws evolved, owned, practised and espoused elsewhere? Is this the reason why more than half of the educational syllabi studied in Africa originate and is developed for other continents and as such is better suited to them and not Africa? Is this, indeed, the reason why like servants doomed only to serve, Africa owns nothing of herself?

Is this curse of enslavement the very reason why Africa is mentally enslaved in more ways than one? Painful as it may be to admit, is this the reason why instead of Africa exploring the liberty of independence, being innovative and daring to recover lost ground, she is rather bound by the excuse that she was once subjected to slave trade? Is this the reason why instead of seeing her every adversity as an opportunity to master her fate and be a giver of solutions to the rest of the world, she is held captive to the ideology that the odds against Africa are disproportionately weightier than those of others and as such, she needs to be treated always with disproportionate leniency? Is this curse, indeed, the reason why Africa, in spite of its phenomenal natural and human capital, remains bound to poverty, death and war? Is this why she also holds to an enslaved mentality, that nothing good comes out of Africa and everything that comes from outside her is superior? Of course, some learned enough to read these questions of mine may vehemently disagree with me, but does the majority of Africa, or your countrymen agree with you or with my vexations?

Is this condemnation to cursed slavery the reason why, without chains and shackles on their feet and in spite of their polished demeanours, Africans are always looked down upon, even though many people of other races will say hand on heart, they condemn any form of racism? But if the hard truth be told, should we not say that many of *"them"* will never consider the African as equal? Is this, by any stretch of the imagination, the reason why it is alright for thousands and perhaps even millions of Africans to die in both secret and open wars that go unreported to the world, yet insane and trivial events of any order one can think of receives the world's undivided attention? Is this the reason why any African with the slightest indication of stirring a mental revolution, boldness and unity among the African people, gets cut down like grass? Or should I rather say, cut down like a slave who talks back to his master or dares to stir dissent amongst his kind?

But, if peradventure the curse of Noah upon Canaan is what has held Africa back this long, then woe is me, for the troubles of my mind have increased. But is not every word of the same Holy Bible true? Does it not say in Jeremiah 31:29 (NKJV):

"In those days they shall say no more: 'the fathers have eaten sour grapes, and the children's teeth are set on edge.'?

And again in Ezekiel 18:20: (NKJV)

"...The son shall not bear the guilt of the father, nor the father, the guilt of the son. The righteousness of the righteous shall be upon himself and the wickedness of the wicked shall be upon himself..."

So I have pondered, if indeed Africa descended from Canaan, why should their iniquities be upon their descendants, and not just upon the former? Couldn't it even be said that the curse of Noah pre-dates the issuance of the Laws of Moses? Many may argue that according to Jewish philosophy, which partly influenced the writing of the Holy Volumes, a man's sons are a continuation of him and to such there can be no end. Very well, then, but why hasn't the new dispensation of the Messiah, Jesus the Christ, annulled such a curse? After all, isn't it written in the New Testament letter to the Galatians 3:13 (NKJV):

> *"Christ has redeemed us from the curse of the law, having become a curse for us, for it is written, 'cursed is everyone who hangs on a tree.'"*

Surely, the Gospel of Christ has seemingly found a greater spreading in Africa than elsewhere, so shouldn't the redemptive work of Christ in Africa's new Christian dispensation bring about her liberation from the curses of old?

Finally, I ask the questions again – is Ham, son of Noah, the lineage from which Africa descended, and if so, is the curse of Noah over Canaan, his grandson, the reason why Africa has remained enslaved, resulting in comparatively minimal economic, social, political, and technological progress to date? Is this the reason why? Is there indeed enough proof, that this is not the case?

God planted the Garden of Eden and Adam was only required to till it. I am tempted to believe when God drove Adam out of the garden, he had no choice but to plant his own garden and then till it. I have often come across only two types of people – those who believe that they are indeed God in the earth, limited by nothing and so, create their own world as such. The other, accepts the task of merely maintaining the world others have created for them with bricks of doctrine and mortars of mental enslavement. Perhaps it is wise, that a man begs God to drive him out of his garden of comfort – only then, can he learn to plant his own.

4

Could It Have Been
Our Independence?

Contrary to the erroneous belief of many that Ghana was the first to gain independence in Africa, historical records show that before Ghana's independence on 6th March, 1957, Sudan, Morocco and Tunisia had gained theirs the year before, in 1956, on 1st January, 2nd March and 20th March, respectively. Before them were Libya *(24th December, 1951)* Ethiopia *(5th May, 1941)*, Egypt *(28th February, 1922)*, South Africa *(31st May, 1910)* and of course the first of them all, Liberia *(26 July, 1847)*. The latest to gain independence was Eritrea from Ethiopia in 1993.

Averaging about fifty-two years of independence each per country across all 54 African nations, it doesn't take long for one to start wondering whether the developments achieved by the majority of African countries to date reflect the number of years they have been independent for. This deserves some consideration since the single most important motivation for such struggles for independence, was so that the African could manage her own affairs. Many are quick to take the defensive side by arguing that it took other *"developed"* countries hundreds of years of independence to achieve their success. I usually respond by arguing that given the era of technological advancement during which most African nations gained their independence, is there any justification for Africa to waste another two hundred or so years, in order to reach the level of development attained by their so called *"developed"* counterparts?

Without doubt, there are and have been glimmers of hope that Africa and her peoples can chart a path of success in their development. Paradoxically, it is also true that many Africans have privately asked themselves if their countries were better off under colonial rule than they are, post-independence. Perhaps, an even bigger question that lurks in the dark, doubting recesses of people's minds is whether or not the attainment of independence is the main reason or one among others, why Africa's development has not really picked up the right pace. You are entitled to disagree – I merely asked a question.

It is, of course, forgivable for anyone to wonder why there ought to be a link between the independence of any African country and their poor performances economically, socially, politically and developmentally. But the question does need to be asked, why so many African countries appeared to have been doing well economically, with stable security and progressive infrastructural developments during their colonial eras and suddenly, since independence, these gains have become retrogressive or, at best, static. Why? Truth is, in some African countries the only still-standing infrastructures evident are those that were put in place by the colonial governments. Shouldn't it make us wonder?

So, the big question is this: did our African leaders take over the management of our countries when they were least prepared for it? Is that why Africa has remained in its state of stagnancy? If one were to take a very critical look across Africa, one should notice with little effort, that a large number of African countries are still being managed or controlled by leaders or political parties largely made up of the *"old stock"* – that is to say, leaders from early independence eras, or at worst, one or two generations down those eras. These are leaders who believe governance is their right and not one of sacrifice and responsibility. Perhaps, they think so because they had to wrestle it from colonial rule, hence establishing within their sub- consciousness minds, a sense of entitlement or the right to *"keep the trophy"* of their struggles. Such leaders tend to believe politics is common sense and not a dedicated vocation requiring any inherent knowledge and professional development. To them, politics is a jungle – what you win by political hunting, you keep by conferred right.

Whichever way we choose to look at it, the question still remains as before – were we as Africans ready, with the depth of knowledge, thoroughness of skill, rigidity of discipline, and the fluidity of creativity, to manage our own countries when we sought and received independence? If by the slightest chance the answer to that question is "no," then, firstly, consideration must be given to the fact that Africa is still largely held under the leadership and systems of such ill-prepared first-independent regimes. Many may argue that the bearers of Africa's bright ideas didn't live long to implement their sterling ideas and I would have also asked, did they foresee their own elimination and plan against it? In fact, one may even argue, yes, they may have passed on, but not their ideas for Africa's greater good – what then, happened to those ideas?

Secondly, it must also be understood, that with the advent of modern technology, such ill-equipped and ill-prepared forms of leadership and their archaic governing systems have become obsolete in the face of today's fast paced global evolution. If this is so, then it seems logical to reason, that Africa is not likely to recover ground or catch up with the rest of the world unless her old, clingy generation of rulers are totally shifted off the scene along with their archaic systems of nation management.

Biblically speaking, it appears to bear resemblance to the episode of Israel's journey in the wilderness under Moses, where a whole generation had to be wiped off the scene, in order to make way for the subsequent better-coached, progress-oriented, fearless and obedient younger generation to enter the Promised Land. Perhaps history isn't a history of relevance, unless it finds ground to be repeated in part, or indeed, in full. But of course, I am no barbarian so I do not propose the loss of lives in my advocacy for *"clearing the threshing floor of old wheat"*. I am simply saying that sometimes, it is helpful to show an uncooperative tenant out the door and unto the lawn, without necessarily thrusting him onto the road and into the path of an oncoming truck.

At times it feels as though logic is defied in the process and perhaps an argument can be made for viewing the preceding questions as follows: When the colonial masters of Africa managed her affairs, they applied structural systems and mechanisms of governing that were direct duplications of those used in their countries of origin. These seemed to have functioned excellently, albeit *to the disadvantage of the indigenous Africans*. Immediately after the respective African countries gained their independence, these colonial governments returned to their home countries and one thing that has been so evident from then until now – is that their home country governing structures and support systems have all evolved progressively and proactively with time. If we Africans, who so vehemently demanded independence and got it had the capabilities to also better the governing and administrative systems left us, why has the evolution of the world along with its modernity and technology, left us the furthest behind?

So, could the problem have been our independence? Is this the reason Africa's progress is stunted? Could the granting of independence to us have caused an obvious loss of power and control over land, resources and human capital for previous colonial governments? Could the impact of these huge losses following independence only be minimized by re-taking control over Africa in ways other than the obviously scorned acts of slavery? Is that the basis for the league of colonial masters creating artificial trade controls contrary to the free-flowing commerce that used to exist between these now-freed colonies and their colonisers? Is the need to regain control, the reason for the sale of economically crippling lifelong loans and other financial agreements to Africa, perpetuating its drug-like addiction as a result? Are these all the result of Africa's independence? If this is the answer and looking at our progress to date, can we then ask the question - have the real costs of independence *(re-colonisation in new forms)* made the opportunity to manage our own African affairs worth it?

It is one of those rare circumstances where the only choice available to a people is between two necessary evils. On one hand, our leaders and their defective systems that are largely driving African countries into the ground, but with little expectation of these leaders willingly letting go their iron grips; on the other hand, the merchants of Africa's "Venice," who have lost power and control by virtue of granting her independence and who now want their pound of flesh, no matter the cost to Africa's vulnerability. To them, her vulnerability must be encouraged, funded and enforced – after all, it's the only way their control and subordination of Africa can be perpetuated.

So, again I ask: is Africa's independence or the price for it the reason or one of the reasons why Africa hasn't progressed much in its development?

I often find I have to defend myself against my African brothers and sisters for asking these indicting questions, which I ask only because I believe they should help us realign our bearings on the journey to bridging the gap between where we are at and where the world is at. I often say to many, even almighty superpower America was partly colonised by Spain and Britain. And so too were Canada, Brazil, Argentina and Malaysia, among others, but these countries have gone a lot further than most African countries since independence and as such, questions ought to be asked how effectively have we in Africa managed our transition from colonies to independent countries.

It just doesn't add up, that so many years after being granted the liberty of adulthood, Africa still depends heavily on the painfully insulting grace of her evicted caretakers. This might be hard to swallow, and I find it so too, being an African myself. Maybe sometimes the truth does not need swallowing as a whole – I choose to chew on these painful truths over time.

I understand that for my many fellow Africans reading this, I may be stepping on your delicate pride. Forgive me, but nevertheless, it is necessary that I do so. Africa's independence struggles, in my opinion, were largely based on emotions. Was the liberty from colonial rule a good thing? Well, I would say undoubtedly it was an excellent blessing. But, of course, the excellence of an idea is quite different from its implementation and its timing. Yes, at the time of our various national independence, we Africans were angry *(an emotion),* that we were being ruled by foreigners in our own land – and justifiably so. Pride swelled within us; pride that said we could do what our then colonial masters did and we could do it better. This meant managing the country and its resources which, in most cases, at the time, was interpreted as basically shipping Africa's resources over to build the native countries of her colonial masters, notwithstanding the fact that they also built some local African infrastructure in the process – is there therefore any surprise, that fifty plus years on, the only national management understood and practiced by most African governments is exactly what they learnt from their colonial masters – shipping off her natural resources to developed countries.

Was the basis of that assessment *(i.e. that we could manage our countries better)* right? No one knows. Did our colonial governments make us privy to the strategies and decision-making processes and techniques with which they ran our countries at the time they did? Or did we simply see the more visible, yet superficial, administrative side of their national administrative prowess and assume that if that was all there was to it, we could do better? What, then, was the basis upon which our spirits were lifted to believe that we could run our countries better than our colonial powers? Has hindsight proved us right or wrong? That spirit was not wrong – I am only questioning the foundations upon which it was based. And if this question feels unjustified, perhaps this would – what were we doing as Africans, before our colonisation?

Whether we choose to face this question today or leave it for posterity to answer, it will have to be faced head-on at some point in our journey as a people. We must ask: what legacy will our independence leave behind? For me, the answer to this question fifty plus years after independence should be a progressive version of the answer given to the same question ten years after independence. So too, the answer given seventy years after independence must be expected to be a progressive addition on those prior to it. It is not enough to simply say that we have *"peace of mind"* or that we have a *"thriving democracy"* or, as the case might be, that we now have our *"own freedom"*. If none of these can be reflected in the continued improvement in the quality of life for the majority of the population in Africa, or in the creation of opportunities for most of her citizenry to realise their potential, then surely such independence hasn't gained us much. Never mind the complex economic models which are used as indicators that we so readily refer to as economic fundamentals – if I called an average man from the streets in Africa, who has the drive to make a living, and asked him what he thought about life in Africa, believe me, his response will trump every big-book analysis of Africa's economic performances.

Did the passion to gain independence blind us to the need to comprehensively plan to secure and consolidate our independence once gained? Or were we economically sabotaged by our colonial masters as a price we had to pay for our gain of independence and their loss of control? And why haven't we risen above it? Even though many African countries today have men and women who have acquired a modern education, it still seems as if Africa is handicapped in its archaic governance and economic management because the systems of government and economic management are still based on models that reflect the inexperience of our first-generation leaders. Or are the new age leaders of Africa also failing because the complexity of sabotage by colonial powers remains and have, perhaps, waxed stronger in complexity over time?

Could it have been our independence that has brought upon Africa its struggle for progress?

5

Could It Have Been
Our Miseducation?

I once watched a documentary about the University of Oxford in England where it was suggested that some form of *"higher education"* was being taught at the school as early as the year 1096. I immediately got onto the internet and Googled *"Higher learning in Africa in year 1096."* The result was exciting, for me at least. There had actually been a university of some sort established in Timbuktu, Mali, in the twelfth century, teaching religion, mathematics, geography and medicine over four degrees called the *"Circle of Knowledge"*, the *"Superior Degree"*, the *"Secondary Degree"*, and the *"Primary Degree."*

At that moment, I felt a sense of pride and excitement to know that Africa also had a higher institution of learning around the same time as such disciplines of study became more established in the Western world. But hold on! Only when I started looking into the distribution of educational institutions from that era to date and the content of our various curricula, did my excitement quickly disappear.

The first question that begs to be asked is this: has Africa been mis-educated? And in order that there should be no doubt at all as to what that means, perhaps it needs a little more clarification. What I am really trying to ask is this: is the overall *content* of Africa's educational curriculum substantively (i) originated in Africa by Africans; (ii) relevant to Africa; and (iii) applicable to Africa's own agenda first *(if there is one)* and then the rest of the world?

It is easy for many to argue that knowledge is universal and I would be naïve to try and dispute that – but then again, I would be naïve too, in assuming that all knowledge is universally relevant. Thinking from these perspectives, it shouldn't be hard to understand why it makes sense that I ask questions such as these: the histories of Africa that Africans study – who wrote them? And if they aren't written by Africans themselves, where lay the vested interests of those who wrote them? After all, history is essentially a recording of the events of the life of a person or people over time, but we must remember that the perspective from which the history of Africa is presented, or any other history for that matter, will be influenced by whether the historian is a coloniser or one of the colonized, indigenous or not. If history then serves as a foundation, helping us in modern times to chart a more successful course into the future than our predecessors did in their time, what proof is there, that all the history we know and those hidden from the Africans, are not as a result, perpetuating the misdirection of Africa's journey through time?

Take for example, the glorious modern economists and political scientists of Africa who have excelled in the study of economics and international relations, whether in Africa or abroad. Consider the many complex and intricately linked modules they study and which eventually they'll apply in their problem-solving roles on behalf of Africa. Now, let's for a moment ask ourselves how many of these modules, schools of thought, principles, analysis, best practices and laws reflect Africa, first and foremost? How many of them reflect Africans as a peculiar kind of people? How many of them reflect Africa as being at a particular point in her evolution? How many reflect Africa as having an entirely different socio-political-cultural composition? Does this therefore, destroy the original validity of the foreign contents of our study as Africans? Or does it place an onus on us as knowledgeable Africans, to always retune our universally acquired knowledge, to reflect the peculiar contexts of Africa?

Take the language of instruction, for example. Many Africans are instructed largely in either English or French. It's easy for one to quickly dismiss my line of questioning here, even before I start, by saying, *"Oh well, only because they are universal languages."* Well, Mandarin of China was never a universal language until recently when everybody else *"needed"* China. But beyond that, here is the point I wish to put across *(one that nonetheless may be rejected outright by some).* Whether in a local or foreign context, the whole essence of being instructed in knowledge is for one to increase in value and make progress either for oneself or nation. If the language that transmits such value-adding knowledge is not one's mother tongue *(which, sadly, more often than not gets reduced to a conversational medium of communication, but not educational)*, isn't it just likely that inherently, a greater value will subconsciously be attached to the language by which value is transmitted? And if so, is it just remotely possible, that a similarly higher sense of value is attributable to the originators of such a language than one's own mother tongue?

Perhaps at this point it will feel less unwelcoming for me to be blunt about a thing or two that we need to further ponder. If a country A, were to develop a body of knowledge largely based on its own circumstances, and if it were able to market that body of knowledge as one that works really well and thus as a result, is able to readily export that body of knowledge for consumption by citizens of countries B, C and D, then we could theoretically *(and maybe practically)* say, that if the consumers of that knowledge in countries B, C and D do not have enough time and resources to first of all synthesise that body of knowledge and make it wholly applicable to their respective countries *(i.e. by first recalibrating the body of knowledge to make it relevant in countries B, C and D)*, then, by and large, the body of knowledge of country A is most likely to be be wholly adopted by B, C and D. Now, country A has, just as a result of this simple but subtle process, created automatic support and following for most of her future interactions that will be based on that body of knowledge as a result of being its originator.

Let's face it; Africa's knowledge should be her responsibility, shouldn't it? So, why hasn't Africa taken responsibility for its own educational needs? Why hasn't she been inspired to strive for higher stakes in the race to be the originator of knowledge, both for her and for the rest of the world? Why is Africa content to be the consumer of most other knowledge and creator of little or none? In an age where information and knowledge are the highest forms of transformative currency, why does it appear as though African governments do not see a paramount need to throw their resources behind the education and mental liberation of their people? Why do we fail to see, that until Africa's population reaches a *critical mass of critically knowledgeable individuals*, all other things such as governance, economy and social development will remain a distant mirage. This lack of foresight is an ongoing reflection of the current critical mass of less than average critical thinkers.

Every so often, I am reminded quite crudely that the majority of the early formal education systems in Africa were set up by the trespassing colonial masters. Fault them as we may, yet at least they saw the value of educating the African in a manner and with a curriculum that not only served and reinforced their presence, but also perpetuated it. Come to think of it, it made sense that the educational systems of colonial powers should serve their interests. Absolutely! What didn't and still hasn't made sense to me in many African countries is – why after independence haven't the majority of our educational systems gained their own independence? Why have we gained political independence but failed to engage in an internal process to liberate our educational systems' enslavement to colonial design? Why has Africa never been able to understand that it takes creativity and critical thinking to build nations and for that matter, refined creativity and ruthless critical thinking? Why, then, haven't we understood the importance of building such creative and critical thinking capacities in our people? Then we can in turn question the errors we so much want to avoid and create from ground up, the glorious countries we so much desire.

Why, even today, do our educational systems consider education as the study of what has been and what already is, rather than *what it could have been if we explored it* or, better still, *what it can be if we create it*? Why should our curricula encourage the already invented reality rather than the inventible imagination? Why don't our educational systems train the minds of our children to explore a future that is yet to be, rather than force them to absorb what we are already living? Why can't learning be centred around finding solutions to problems the world has not yet dreamed of, rather than focusing on solutions already known? Why can't we change our educational contents from what the world says is right, to what we deem is best for Africa? Why doesn't it bother us that we are the only continent not widely represented in the world's leading schools of thought? Why haven't we yet understood that creating knowledge equates to being the first-line beneficiary of the rewards of that knowledge? Why can't our politicians understand that winning the global race is not about mining raw materials but rather, cultivating high-quality brain societies?

Perhaps it is daring to say that we as Africans short-changed ourselves at independence, both individually and as a continent, when all we settled for was the physical expulsion of our colonial masters, whilst the machinery and infrastructures of education that controlled our thinking within those so-called freedoms remained and have now become the machinery that still binds us to the old whims.

Today, the race for world superiority is really all about who can be at a certain point in the future before everybody else gets there. The rest of the world understands that huge leverage abounds to whoever arrives first. Africa needs to realize, that of the many things she is blessed with, neither her natural resources nor her rich culture can take her into that future, let alone give her a high standing in the rankings. It takes one thing and one thing only – minds trained and minds willing to travel outside the boxes of human reality. *It takes creative knowledge.*

So, in times past when educational systems were not under our own control, were we being mis-educated? And when we finally took control of our own nations, did we mis-educate ourselves and are we still doing so? It should be clear by now I hope, that if we have indeed mis-educated ourselves, then chances are that the next generations are likely to apply the same modules of miseducation to the future of Africa. Can it be shortened? Can it be avoided? Only if we recognize first that there has been miseducation. But beyond that, such a change must be enforced with ruthless radicalism.

A friend of mine posed me a question recently. I was sure I had heard it before but just couldn't remember from whom or where. The question was this: *why is Africa still hungry in the midst of plenty?* My response to him was equally short: *because Africa's hunger is one of food, not knowledge!*

So I end where we started – is the miseducation of Africa, whether by herself or by others, the reason why she remains largely behind time on the clock of development? Is it the reason why some still see our own educational systems as subservient to those we have come to cherish as the *"Ivy League"* of all education? Is our miseducation the reason why our leaders, who have been educated in some of the world's best schools and possessing some of the world's best non-contextual knowledge, come back and realize they are failures in the African context? Is our miseducation the reason why the world has moved on from agrarian, past industrial, and is now in the information age and yet Africa is largely still caught between the agrarian and industrial ages? Is our miseducation the reason why African leaders are failing to see that the real driving force of the world today is creative value-adding minds and not finite natural resources?

Could it, by any chance be our miseducation?

6

Could It Have Been
Genetic or Cultural?

Outside religion and politics, perhaps culture is one of the most sensitive things about which to talk to most fellow Africans. I believe, without a doubt, that this section will raise some of the most troubling of my questions yet. But does it make sense to raise the issues on culture alongside genetic considerations? For me, the depth with which either is embedded in any human psyche makes them difficult to separate.

Is the genetic and cultural constitution of Africans the reason for her not-too-impressive progression?

There are, no doubt, African cultural practices and embedded natures that have not helped our progression as a people. I am certain every African country would find a few of those on its own doorsteps. But people can change their cultural views, although I am not necessarily saying they should. But at least it is a hopeful feeling to know that if an ingrained cultural practice is becoming unhelpful to progress, it can, with effort, be changed. My doubt is that the same can be said easily of inherent genetic patterns.

Now, some world-acclaimed and even Nobel prize-winning geneticists like Dr James Watson have gone so far as to say that, genetically speaking, the African's intelligence genome empirically makes him or her below par to other races. Don't worry, I don't believe all of his findings myself. And yes, he has been slammed internationally for subtly inciting *"scientific racism."* I am sure there is a high probability that you, reading up to this point, would have also considered such an assertion to be racist. But the question is - are all men born equal? I personally believe so. I do not believe, however, that our human or racial constitutional make-up is evenly distributed. My understanding of all men being created equal is that we each possess, whether individually or along racial groupings, unique sets of abilities and human functionalities, some of which we excel in more than other people or groups of people. It is these balances in our strengths and weaknesses, as compared to others, that make us equal. In other words, there may be some natural instincts or capabilities that the African may excel in, which other races will not and vice versa. I feel it is these intra-racial or intra-personal disparities in positives and negatives that make us all equal. The real progression from there onwards is in how we use our positives to excel above others.

As an African, I should naturally feel offended by the comments made by Dr Watson, but I had to check myself and give equity to my reasoning. No, I certainly don't agree outright with his assertion, but perhaps we need to respectfully accept that he based such a comment on empirical scientific evidence. Then we must ask, on what do we as Africans base our denials and disagreements? Given our naturally vested interest to justify our version of the truth, if we too carried out such types of research, we could possibly disprove Dr Watson and many other such wild findings? Or would we, perhaps, also discover equally demeaning genetic traits in other races, not for the purposes of antagonism but to broaden the scope of scientific knowledge? +

Let us assume for a moment, and with good justification, that the African has no genetic defects. Shall we then ask the bluntest of questions: if you were to look around, wherever you are, whilst reading this very sentence, about what percentage of the things you see around you were conceived, invented, designed, built or made functional by Africans? In my estimation, problem solving is all about creativity – the ability to *"create"* the hitherto non-existent or to modify the already existing thing for relevant practical use. There will always be problems, but why has Africa not been able to find solutions to some of its oldest, most common and recurring ones? Countries like Malaysia and Singapore used to be third world too. So why have they managed to achieve a somewhat *"developed"* status over a shorter period of time, than many similar countries in Africa? Again, we remember Japan being very much levelled to the ground after heavy bombings during World War II, yet today it stands tall, a power player in many respects. I am sure there are many other examples of countries, which have evolved into better states of existence after one form or the other oppression or annexation. Why have they been able to substantively think themselves out of their previous negative situations and Africa largely hasn't done so?

Perhaps it has nothing to do with our genetic design and everything to do with our aged traditions or cultures. Is that really the cause of Africa's woes? Is it culture that tells us that it is grossly disrespectful to question seniors in age and experience, whether they are wrong or right? Is it this same tradition that grows into a monster, making us fail to demand accountability from our many corrupt African leaders? Shall we say, it is tradition that tells us that certain occupations, indulgences, levels of wealth, exposures, ways of thinking and so on are only reserved for certain persons who are predestined to have them? Could it be, that the same social stratifying culture prevents the young girl or the exceptionally bright village boy from exploring their inherent and obvious abilities to find answers to questions never before asked simply because they have been told by culture, that their line of passion is not in keeping with their social origin or status? Maybe it is this same culture that kills a multiplicity of talent and leads an adult African accountant, painter or gardener to believe that he or she is good for nothing and must not explore other latent talents other than what his profession and societal stereotypes define him to be? Could it be?

Shall we say it is tradition that incessantly tells us that *"curiosity killed the cat?"* Is it the same tradition that sets up African parents to automatically silence their enquiring children with the ever popular phrase *"stop asking too many questions?"* We may ask, if embedded within different African folklores, are subtle but potent anecdotes that unknowingly stifle our inquisitiveness and hence, our ability to explore the world around us? This might have contributed to us not being explorers, discovering new worlds or being creators of new things - and therefore not being numbered among the pacesetting innovators of our time. Did our tradition fail to tell us, however, that although curiosity may have killed the cat, knowledge certainly brought it back to life? So just what is it - a genetic disorder or a self-destructive culture or tradition?

But then we must also ask about indiscipline. Yes, the indiscipline that sees legislative institutions built on exactly the same laws as successful countries worldwide - the very laws which fail to function equitably and progressively in Africa. Why? Because the undisciplined guardians of those laws in Africa, while seeing to it they are enforced among the citizens, exempt themselves and instead create their own laws. Which exactly is it - genetic or cultural defects? Yes, I mean the same indiscipline that allows us to seek internal and external consensus on the best and most comprehensive economic policies for our African countries' success and then, not follow them to the letter, thus perpetuating the cycles of economic failures. So, which exactly is it – genetic or cultural flaws? Maybe it is none of the above.

Could it merely be the indiscipline that permeates even our so-called fragile democracies? Yes, the undisciplined African democracies which endorse politicians to use their fellow citizens to gain votes and then trample them underfoot, often capitalizing on their depravities by buying off their victims with mere morsels of lofty promises?

But how about the even basic indiscipline of the ordinary citizen who disobeys traffic regulations whether or not he is being observed; who discards trash and personal filth in public space; jumps queues; shows total disregard for time; who displays rude customer service attitudes, and indeed all the rest of everyday indiscipline we see around us? Which exactly is it – genetic or cultural shortcoming?

How about the *"African Greed"* we so often talk about? Is that a genetic or cultural dysfunction that has held Africa back as a people? Are all Africans really greedy or does it all start in political office? Could this be the Holy Grail to Africa's permanent recovery if we were certain about its cultural or genetic origins? Why is the African greed so focused on making individuals the most financially and politically powerful amongst their peers, whereas the greed of other nations is biased towards making their countries financially, militarily, politically or technologically superior to other nations? How about the greed that permits a humble man to be content with his loaf of bread until he rises to a position of power, then suddenly desires the bread and meat of an entire nation and is prepared to kill to retain his power and ill-gotten wealth?

What shall we then say about the greed that drives the hearts of men towards ungodly insanity – to take up arms against their own brothers, to rape their mothers and wives, burn their infants, and feed the bodies of their fathers to beasts, just so they alone can own a shallow valley of gold or diamonds? Is this greed of genetic origin or cultural cultivation?

Is it a natural genetic or cultural deviation that inherently programs certain Africans to believe it is impossible for us all to prosper simultaneously? Why is there an inherent subconscious programming, that in order to do well, someone else ought to go down and if they don't, then they ought to be forced down? Shall we be quick to conclude that this deviation only applies to Africa's leaders? Then perhaps the question to ask is: are our leaders not taken from amongst us? Or perhaps we should say, sarcastically, that fate has a way of selecting for leadership only those men and women from amongst us who bear the seeds of evil greed. Shall we say so?

Indeed, many have pondered why African countries have struggled for many decades to come together as a united front and by so doing become one of, if not the strongest unified force ever in world history. Could it be because, no matter how hard we try, there will always be some amongst us whose inherent propensity for personal greed will remain the suicidal enemy within, that the enemies of African unity will depend on to foil our efforts?

I have often heard the derogatory statement made, even by Africans themselves, that you can take the African out of the bush but you can't take the bush out of the African. Sad as it is, shall we then also say that you can take the African out of his cultural roots or genetic origins but you can't take his culture or genes out of him?

So again albeit sadly, I ask the question: is the genetic or cultural constitution of the African the reason for her unimpressive evolution since independence? Are the consistently displayed indiscipline and corruption we see in Africa, stemmed from or culture or genes?

For many Africans who are highly religious, perhaps the question that will contend with our faith is this – if peradventure these were all defects in our genes, did God give us such genes with deliberate intent? But surely there are Africans who do not exhibit these extremities of indiscipline or greed – or are these latter breed of Africans rather the deviations from norm? Would that, for instance, explain why the majority of African leaders in power are a corrupt version of their breed? Should this suffice to conclude that these concerns have nothing to do with our genes? Is it then all a cultural affair? Is that the reason why some Africans, who have the opportunity to be immersed in other cultures, change in their ways of thinking and outlook on life? But how about the many others who are similarly exposed to these different cultures and yet do not change in their thinking or out-look? What exactly is it – our genes or our culture?

Again, I ask, could it be our genetic or cultural constitutions that have held Africa back?

7

Could It Have Been
Our Religious Immersion?

It is my prayer that you do not commence reading this section with anger or disgust already in your mind merely because I may by my questions imply, that religion, especially the Christian religion, may be part of the reason why Africa hasn't progressed. But come, let us reason together. That's what I ask, for I too am a Christian. I do not believe that our Christianity should in any way inhibit the rightful progress of humanity, especially Africans. For what worth is it, if the liberating works of Jesus the Christ on the cross of Calvary should only be experienced as a tingling in our ears and an illusionary expectation in our daily lives but never a communal manifestation of a life worthy of a king's children. The apostles before us tested and experienced the tangible spectrum of liberty in Christ, wherefore Paul the apostle wrote in Philippians 4:11-13:

> "......*I know* how to be abased, and *I know* how to abound.
> Everywhere and in all things I have learned both to be full
> and to be hungry, both to abound and to suffer need. I can
> do all things through Christ who strengthens me."

Shall we not say then, that if we be followers of Jesus the Christ, then it is NOT of God that we should only be abased but that we ought also to experience abounding? Is this the case with the majority in Africa with a largely Christian background? Shall we also not say then, that if we be followers of Jesus the Christ, then all things must work together for our good?

Various statistics estimate that Christians form approximately 50% to 60% of the African population and it only takes a glance at the continent to realize how much of a boom Christianity has enjoyed in this century, notwithstanding the persecution of Christians in some African countries. So, indeed, Christianity does have enough numbers to transform the direction of Africa.

Here comes the question then – has Christianity in Africa failed Africans? Is Christianity the reason why Africa has seemingly regressed rather than progressed?

I do not ask this question to stir up passions; I ask so that our Christianity can stand tall and defend itself and its power to transform, to restore and to establish. I have intentionally chosen not to dwell on the anthropologies surrounding the introduction of Christianity to Africa. Many argue that Christianity was brought to Africa by the West and I easily diffuse such arguments by asking – how about the Ethiopian eunuch talked about in the book of Acts chapter 8, who, on his way back to Ethiopia from Jerusalem, was preached the Gospel by Philip and baptized? Did he not carry the gospel back to Ethiopia and to Candace, the queen of Ethiopia? What matters however, is that Christianity has now developed so powerfully in Africa that the former importers of this religion have now become the bene-factors and exporters to the rest of the world. But if it is the same principles of Christianity that transformed the fortunes of the countries who presumably spread Christianity to sub-Sa-haran Africa; if it is the same Christianity they practised as we now do in Africa, and if Africa's Christianity has today become stronger, more vibrant and more evident than that of the former exporters of it, how come its transformative power is not being reflected in Africa?

The Holy Bible does say in James 2:26 that "*faith without works is dead*", meaning that our works should be proof that our faith is alive. So I ask – does Africa have enough works to show for her fiery faith? If not, is it an indictment that our faith is dead? But how can it be so, seeing that the evident rise in the Christian faith in Africa has been unprecedented? Is there, then, a miss-ing link between our Christian faith and the glorious works that should reflect it? I refer to such works as the total destruction of poverty, of completely eradicating religious and ethnic violence, the achievement of financial prosperity and a good standard of living for all its citizens. Why are the works not reflecting the faith?

To repeat, James 2:26 tells us that *"faith without works is dead"*, meaning that our faith is only alive when it is backed up by "works". So I ask – has Christianity in Africa really given life to our faith through the use of our brains and hands to mould the better Africa and the positive future we believe in? Or, very unashamedly, has our Christian faith made us prone to laziness, thus making it look like faith in the promises of our God yields no results, especially for Africa? Have we failed in our responsibilities as Christians to work with the mind of God and, by so doing, bring into manifestation those things which, by faith, we have believed to be rightfully ours?

Could it be the case that the creative power of Christianity has been wrongly taught to us as consisting only of prayer? Could this be the reason why we pray for Africa and our individual progress, yet expect a manifestation of the same not by our human efforts, collaborating with heaven, but by supernatural occurrences only? Is this thus the manner in which our wrongly taught Christianity has held us back? Or have we wrongly been taught that *"it is ALL the WILL of God"*, in which case we have no role to play in heaven's predestined occurrences? But I ask yet again – is God such an unjust God, that He will grant to us the power of *will*, to make choices between the things we hope for and the things we have faith in, and yet deny us the chance to partake in the exercising of our wills to manifest faith? Will God be responsible then, for moulding our hands for laziness?

Is this inherent nature of our Christian religion holding us back, so that we do everything it admonishes us to do except the one thing that matters most – to work proactively. And why don't we work? Is it simply because it is the *"will of God"* or better put, because *"it is in God's hands"*? Indeed, what man will dare wrestle a thing from God's hands? Or perhaps what manner of man won't justify his voluntary incapacitation on the basis that his will is lesser than the will of God? Is it not insulting, in the least, to paint a picture of God as one who gives us a will to exercise, yet prevents us from doing so? Is it not insulting to think that the same God of incontestable creativity, who created us in His own image, will deny us the ability to exhibit the same level of creativity in the earth, merely on the basis that *"all things are in His hands"*?

But I ask this: why does God say to Abram in Genesis 17:1 *"walk **before** me…"*, and in Micah 6:8, *"……walk humbly **with** your God"*; yet, to Israel in Deuteronomy 13:4, He commands *"You shall walk **after** the Lord …"*? Surely, it is to reveal to us that there are times when God requires us to lead the way *(before Me), to* chase our visions, so He can back us up with His grace. At other times, He requires that we partner with Him *(with your God)* side by side, in which case He supports us just as we support His manifestation here on earth. Still, at other times, He expects us to follow His lead *(after the Lord)* and walk behind him as He leads us into the future that only His omnipresence knows. But under no circumstances, in the practice of our faith with God, does He require us to leave everything in His hands or to His will alone – never.

So, could it be that God has done His part, by endowing Africa with almost 40% of the world's gold, approximately 73% of the world's diamonds, an estimated 75% of its cobalt, nearly 30% of its potential hydroelectric power, close to 50% of its manganese, and millions of acres of untilled fertile farmland, as well as other natural resources? And yet, could it be that we have hidden behind the cloak of religion and subconsciously expect God, besides providing us with these resources, to descend to earth, cook and feed us with its blessings too?

Undetectable immediately by the untrained eye, the Christian church in Africa is one of, if not the, most powerful institutions, much more powerful than any political institution. It is the one institution that depends most on the physical gathering of many, to inspire oneness through fellowship. It is the one institution that guarantees the coming together of the spirit, the soul and the bodies of millions of people weekly, thereby creating the greatest opportunity to influence both the conscious and subconscious states of many. Christianity in Africa is the only institution that has the ability to justify its actions with the backing of God, who permeates all other earthly authorities. That's how powerful the Christian church in Africa is. The question then arises: has Christianity in Africa therefore failed Africa by emphasizing only the knowledge of the Bible and none other? Is that the reason why the millions of Christians in Africa know everything the Holy Bible says but nothing about how the world around them works? Yes, many will argue, the Bible admonishes in 2 Timothy 2:15:

> *"Study to show yourself approved unto God, a workman that need not be ashamed, rightly dividing the word of truth".*

But did *"our"* Christianity fail to teach our people, that the *"studying"* referred to is as much about the kingdom of God, as it is about the world in which we are expected to operate the kingdom's mandate? How justified is it, that a man will be admonished to study *"a way of life"* but not *"the environment"* in which he is expected to live that life daily?

Has Christianity largely failed Africa by emphasizing the casting out of demons alone and not inspiring the exploitation of creative talents that God has deposited in us? Surely if all our handicaps are caused by demons and spirits, there is no justification whatsoever, to engage the deep critical thinking of the African or his creative intellect in finding solutions to our problems, but rather, employ an equally spiritual engagement as a vehicle to solve our problems. And if such is the case, always, then it is logical that the spirit of the African finds more opportunity to exercise itself than his or her mind does. How, then, can we prove that our God is a God of creation if we ourselves are not inspired to create continuously? Does the ever-so-creative God not say in 1 John 4:17, "...*as He is in heaven, so are we here on earth?*" Has Christianity therefore largely failed Africa by emphasizing ONLY the word of God and not inspiring us to great heights of creativity and wider learning? Consider the entirety of the Bible's New Testament – were there not twelve Disciples of Christ? How is it then, that almost all the books of this Testament were written and preserved by only the most learned amongst them?

Is it worth considering, that if the apostles had not been learned enough to preserve the events and teachings of the Christ, our Christianity would not have evolved? Was Moses, who wrote the Torah, not learned in languages, the astrology of the Pharaohs and the royal art of scribes? Was he not further instructed in the art of leadership by Jethro his father-in-law, a non-Israeli priest? Did Jethro not teach Moses the wisdom of setting up a government with different arms, which today, forms the model of all government administration structures? Yet, is it not the thorough non-Judeo, non-Christian understandings of how the systems of the world works, that set these great men apart as the best candidates for God's use, in capturing, preserving and propagating the works of God's kingdom? Has Christianity largely failed Africa by emphasizing ONLY prayer and not inspiring the church after praying, to engage in mental creativity and critical thinking? Is it not the same God that beckons us to come reason together with Him? Is it not His wisdom that inspired His servant to write in Proverbs 23:7, "*For as he thinks in his heart, so* *is he…".? Does the Lord therefore, in spite of His many blessings towards us, not require us, to not only pray, but THINK?

Has the Christian religion, or the way it has been taught, failed Africa because it has not instilled in its followers the understanding of faith as a two way street – that God has upheld and will continue to uphold His part of the deal and we, doing our part by working, does not diminish our faith in Him but rather reveals it? Perhaps, the African church needs to re-educate us that as long as we remain beings each possessing a spirit, soul and body, our wholeness, whether perceived in faith or reality, can never be achieved solely by spiritual means. Instead, it requires the working of all three dimensions– (i) the Spirit – God's presence and interaction (ii) the soul – our thinking minds and deep emotions and (iii) the body - our hands that create the manifested amalgamation of God and man's mind on earth.

God, in His infinite wisdom created the sun and the moon, to which He assigned rules so that neither of these heavenly bodies has need of human involvement in order to work to perfection. However, the same God who planted a not so complex garden for Adam required him to *"till the ground" or work it,* in order that its excellence be maintained. We must ask ourselves, whether God had a good reason to place the same divine degree of importance on <u>man's mental and physical work,</u> as He did on the heavenly rules that keep the sun, the moon and the stars in their glorious orbits.

I am of great, though pardonable hope that those of other faiths reading this book will understand that I have only chosen to speak on Christianity because it is what I know.

So finally, I ask the question again: could Africa's immersion in the Christian religion have been the reason for our failure to develop as a people?

8

Could It Have Been
the Superpowers?

Whenever one hears the popular story of David and Goliath, one automatically knows that David triumphs. What escapes us as a result of the heart-warming power of that story is that there are many other scenarios like that, where the "David" is brutally crushed or annihilated –only such stories don't get told often.

In my opinion, there are only two ways in such a relationship for Goliath to remain overpowering – either he limits the growth of David in stature and wisdom, or he himself continually grows mightier and wiser than David. You would imagine then, that the best approach would be to do both – that is, for Goliath to keep growing more powerful and wiser, whilst simultaneously weakening David's ability to grow mentally and physically.

The question is: is that what the world's superpowers did to Africa? Is Africa a victim of an eternalized superiority agenda? Is that why Africa has remained where it is? Is it a result of an agenda by the nations referred to as *"superpowers,"* to remain superior in every form of power? After all, something must remain small for something else to be considered big in comparison. Yes? Is it deliberate or is that just the way some things are meant to be?

There is sufficient evidence that the founding fathers of America had already laid out detailed plans on how they intended to dominate the world and so too had the British Empire long before many African countries begun seeking independence. Africa was certainly one of the most vulnerable acquisitions in those strategic plans. Ever since then, it appears that large corporations and business empires of these superpower countries have carried out slow, systematic, but sustained piece by piece "acquisitions" of Africa. Without being excessively nice about it, I am sure many have wondered if this is the reason why Africa does not get the international support it reasonably requires developing to the level matching her years of independence. Is this a strategy to keep Africa disadvantaged in order for the *"rulers of the world"* to be at an advantage? Is that the real agenda behind the Economic Partnership Agreements between Africa and Europe, proposing different trading terms for Africa than exists for their own regional partners? Could this *"keep-Africa-low"* agenda be a principal strategy consideration for the regular Bretton-Woods gathering of the world's most powerful people to formulate different rules for different intra-national commercial and financial dealings?

Is that the reason China is largely trading its cheap labour, non-durable products and cheap binding loans all over Africa in return for longer term, largely more valuable oil, minerals and green resources? Or is that the business case for America establishing its Africa Command Centres to be a *"gentle reminder"* of military intimidation – a reminder to Africa's individual countries to be wary about saying *"no"* when they are required to say *"yes"* and vice versa? Is this the intricate web of commercial entrapment that has kept Africa at her low ebb to date?

Couldn't one argue that the once *"Asian Tiger"* nations experienced the same web of suffocation, but found their way around it? Is Africa any different? If not, why can't she turn her fortunes around in the very manner the Asians did? Or, perhaps, putting it bluntly, Africa has just been cornered by the league of superpower nations into being their *"resource annex."*

The World Bank provides financial help to Africa, but at what long term economic expense? Is it at the expense of African countries exchanging their economic sovereignty for the adopted policies of the World Bank? How about the International Monetary Fund *(IMF)* and the International Finance Corporation *(IFC)* and all the other institutions like them *(some, never to be known publicly),* that together remain brothers in arms? Are they not banded together with the one aim of making their "real" *(industrialised nations)* owners profits at the expense of the borrowing nations? Are there, indeed, not some among this pack of financial wolves that lure African countries into the trap of *"death loans"*? Are there not others whose aim after the lure, is to bind African countries to the stake of economic policy conditionalities embedded in such loan agreements? Are there not yet others that specialize in strangling these already bound African countries, with repayment and exit terms that perpetually dry up the financial blood of these borrowing nations for several generations? Beneath the shields of diplomacy and tact under which these facilities are contracted, is the real agenda not the introduction of as many African countries to the vicious cycle of total dependence? But I ought not to assume this is the case, so I ask – could these be the reasons why Africa remains economically crippled?

Perhaps we should reason wisely, that there are many ways in which the world's superpowers can manipulate the growth and development of Africa without necessarily employing direct economic mechanisms. Should I then ask the question: how about the grabbing of large parcels of Africa's lands in the name of everything but long-term strategic economic and social take-over? Yes, how about the grabbing of lands either resource rich or merely central to future population frontiers by foreign conglomerates, empires, governments and so-called international bodies in the name of *"supporting development"*? Are these the reasons for Africa's hijacked growth? Is it not the case that *"he who owns the land, owns the people of the land*?" Is it not wisdom, that without lands, there will be no people and without a people, there is therefore not a nation? Doesn't the man who owns a land, also own with it every benefit of wealth and power that comes out of it, whether by occupation or use? Is this the reason why Africa is handicapped? Shall we as Africans be warned that if we ignore this, a time comes when Africans will live on their lands, not as the owners of it, but as wanderers and disenfranchised citizens?

Permit me however to play the righteous advocate of the devil by asking – if Africa's lands were not being taken from her, what would she have used them for? For the many years we have had our own lands, what have we used them for? What are we doing with our own lands, that will make their subtle or aggressive takeovers by corporations and governments who have proved efficient in the use of their own lands, appear unfair and unjustified? Do the tenets of economics we all subscribe to globally not advocate the transfer of resources or capital from non-productivity to productivity?

But surely, if lands cannot be taken from Africans, isn't the next best thing to deny her the power to control productivity from those lands? I am simply asking a question. Would that be the agenda for the forceful introduction of Genetically Modified Organism (GMO) foods? These are foods that have their yields altered from natural to scientific, so that the productivity of such foods no longer depend on the fertility of the land and the virility of crops, but on the power of the science that created them. Ultimately, the owners of these sciences become gods who control the vegetative reproduction of crops. Is it not the case that once introduced, future crop growths become controlled not by the farmers who labour in modesty, but by the greedy gods who seek to own the world? And indeed if a man should own the belly of a nation, does he not own the kings of that nation too?

Is it simply because Africa *(whether she knows it or not)* carries the potential to be self-sustaining in her agricultural needs as well as be the continent on which the world may eventually depend on for its food? Is that why such a potential ought to be destroyed now together with everything in its path? Or is it simply because Africa's eventual actualization of agricultural self-sustenance threatens the export profits of superpower subsidized farms, laboratories and processed food factories? Are these likely effects on the superpowers the reason Africa *"must be made"* to fail in the area of its most potential competitive advantage – agriculture? Are these the reasons why Africa has woefully failed to surmount the scourge of importing food, despite her natural capacity to feed herself and the rest of the world?

I have often asked myself this: why do the most repressive rulers and governments in Africa attract the most foreign business and in many cases, the most financial, albeit not very obvious, backing from super powers?" Why? Is it because it presents the easiest and most secure form of control – that is, first divide them using their own lines of discord, then use them against one another in order to control their nations? Or is it easiest for nations to cover their tracks of stealing from Africa by using the justification of humanitarian aid – that is, to steal 100% and return 5% in the form of aid? Is it because such violence-based regimes provide two-fold joys for the superpower nations? On the one hand, it keeps the people of Africa focused on fighting one another thus providing a distraction from the looting vans, planes and ships that cart away her resources daily? And on the other hand, it guarantees secure avenues to milk whatever is left of Africa's economic cows, through re-construction and re-building programmes which use Africa's own labour and natural resources, but, in the end, require her to make exorbitant payments or otherwise agree to be bound into eternally crippling borrowing arrangements.

All I wish to do is ask the question: could this be the reason why Africa has remained as the least developed continent in the world? Is it like this, so that in such repressive regimes the peace needed to extensively think and plan development is replaced with thinking and planning only for survival? Is it like this, so that in such violent conflicts the trust needed to bond the synergies of a people for progressive work is replaced with vile suspicion and hatred? Is it like this, so that in such despotic environments the resources needed to mobilize growth is used in buying arms, happily supplied by the same superpowers? Is that the reason why Africa has remained bound perpetually in the vicious cycle of violence-fed underdevelopment?

Certainly, the media is one of the greatest powers in the world, but greater still are those that have the means to give any media its global reach. The people who have such power also have the ability to effortlessly create consensus as well as manipulate the sustenance of such consensus among a given population. The question is: has this kind of media power been used to stunt Africa's growth? Is it not just possible, that worldwide media channels have been, are being, and can be used to shape both consensus and consent for agendas that are not likely to be in the eventual interest of those giving such consent? Is it not possible that worldwide media, using the right psychology, design and technology have the power, if applied subtly but consistently over time, to make Africans worldwide believe untruths about themselves?

Isn't it a fundamental reality that one's image, in the eyes of others, substantively shapes the basis and conditions under which others deal with us? Is it a wonder, then, that it plays to the advantage of the so-called superpowers to portray the image of Africa as one filled with barbarism, incompetence, filth, death, starvation – everything but that which is human? Indeed, would a lender with good credit deal with a perceived barbarian in the same manner as he would with a "civilized" individual? Could Africa change this negative image about herself if she had the means, of also controlling the creation and reach of her own media? Is the possibility of positively re-educating Africa via media one of the reasons why the powers that be, will do whatever is necessary to block brave African countries from progressing beyond the launch and total ownership of small- to medium-capability satellites?

How about this concern regarding language which is as old as age itself? How about the indiscriminate subtleness with which everything negative is cunningly woven into the colour black? Shall we say it has perhaps been the most successful psychological campaign to have ever been unleashed against Africa and indeed her black race? Has it not gotten to the point that Africans themselves have, without obvious notice, trained their own reflexes and subconscious natures to align with this subtle deception that everything black is evil, incapable, and inferior? Could this be the greatest war superpower nations have fought against Africa – to make her people believe that nothing good can come out of them and for that matter, any African? Could this be the reason why Africa, after all her independence struggles, still largely feels more secure as a dependant than she does believing herself to be her own solution? Could this be the reason why Africa trails behind?

Certainly, the questions raised here do not even scratch the surface of the complexities that the world's superpowers are engaged in where Africa is concerned. Nevertheless, the question eventually still needs to be asked: are their activities and plots, whatever they are, the reasons why Africa remains comparatively stagnant in her overall development as a continent?

Could the limiting works of superpower nations, be the reason why Africa is where it is - stagnant?

9

Could It Have Been
A Different Africa?

We must have gone wrong somewhere. Hard as it may be to swallow, hypocrisy will only bury us alive if all we do is stand back and direct our plight away from the very obvious truth we wished never was – that indeed, we must have got it wrong somewhere. And whether we find where we missed it, as a continent, as nations or as individuals, one thing is certain – we must chart a different path from the one we've trod these many wasted years. God, unlike in the case of the Israelites in the wilderness, will not, for a second time, scream at us as He did Moses, saying: *"You have circled this mountain for too long; turn around and head northward."*

How, then, shall we chart our new course?

Shall we now bite the bullet and face the truth, that we are a different breed of people, with different strengths and peculiar natural tendencies; and that the off-the-shelf democracies, textbook-governance philosophies and standardized economic policies don't work for us because they were neither developed by us, for us, with our input, nor for our end advantage? Shouldn't we now damn the consequences of such deviations and look to drive our nations and continent forward the "African way"? Indeed, what is wrong with having an African governance philosophy or an African economic school of thought? What is wrong with us having a *(eventually)* tried, tested and established African democracy model or indeed an African political doctrine?

Shall we not now dare enough to explore new discoveries, make mistakes, persist, and make some more mistakes if necessary, until we find our own African way that works? Shall we not be determined to write our own histories and by that, realign our inspirations and our lessons for a brighter future? Shouldn't we now mould our own education system that recognizes the peculiarity of our African nature, the stage we are at in our history and where we wish to be? Shouldn't our education be one that makes us relevant to African needs first and foremost, then beyond that, significant to the rest of the world? Shouldn't this be an education rooted in the pride that Africa is NOT to be seen only as a dark continent but one capable of producing knowledge that the world can follow? Shouldn't this be an education that teaches us that every problem Africa has, ought to be solved by us, not merely for its sake, but because every such problem, at whatever level, is an opportunity for great wealth, worthy of exploitation by Africans?

Yes, the wealth of learning, the wealth of leveraging increased problem-solving skills and, by all means, the financial wealth derived from commercializing practical knowledge therefrom to the rest of the world. Perhaps, it is about time our African leaders are forced to realize that in the dispensation of our modern times, nations no longer grow superior by virtue of the tonnes of gold stored or arms stockpiled, but by the critical mass of quality human brains functioning optimally within our countries. It is about time our leaders and Africa's people realize that development no longer means the mere building of roads and dams, but the mass refinement and emancipation of the minds of Africans to attain to the highest level, so that they grasp and embrace not only current, but also future aspirations. Only then can we, as a continent, find innovative ways to position ourselves in the future before others arrive – that should be our development agenda re-defined.

Maybe then, Africa will begin to turn out for the better or maybe not. I do not know. What I do know is that we cannot stand still or move in directions contrary to the modern world. I could be wrong, perhaps, I could be very right – you are the judge.

A second time, I ask: how, then, shall we chart our new course?

Shall we suppress our disorderliness and do all we can to become more disciplined? After all, it is not beyond us or impossible, is it? So, should we then do whatever we possibly can to become more disciplined? Shouldn't our leaders be disciplined enough to demand the same degree of discipline or higher from their subordinates and they, in turn, from the citizenry? Maybe we should.

Shouldn't we, as individual nations of Africa, be disciplined enough to search for, find and focus on the few but critical drivers of success in our individual societies and to forcefully promulgate them instead of compelling our countries to follow political agendas, not because they have any good to offer but rather, because they are either political-party designed to counter opposition party agendas or because they are the resolves of greedy dictators? Maybe we should.

Shouldn't we be disciplined enough to realise that the world today is driven by technology which is not slowing down but continues to become more complex and will very soon replace *"the natural way of doing things"*? And shouldn't we therefore be disciplined enough to learn most eagerly from countries who have gone ahead of us in technology, not in the manner that allows such learning to enslave us, but that they serve as sparks of inspiration for finding our own path in the shortest time frame? Maybe we should.

Shouldn't we be disciplined enough to manage our priorities along national, not political lines of thought, and follow our strict economic plans to cut down on spending where we need to or to avoid excessive borrowing where it is most prudent? Don't we need to focus less, sometimes, on *"textbook economic indicators"* and more on delivering practical value to our citizens so as to have long-term impacts that our posterity can also enjoy? Maybe we should.

Maybe, then, Africa will begin to turn out for the better; or maybe not. I do not know. What I do know is that indiscipline at any level only has the power to diminish our good efforts and multiply our inefficiencies where they exist. You be the judge.

And for the third time, I ask: how, then, shall we chart our new course?

Should we do away with running our countries, and indeed Africa, without modern, functionally accountable systems because such status quos allow us to feed our corruption, our greed and our thievery rather than reward the hopes, labours and sacrifices of our citizens? Should we replace party political mediocrity with systems enshrined in law that ensure that, at all times, choices that deliver national value are given a fairer chance than fulfilments that satisfy political egos? Should we replace ethnically inclined preferences with systems that inherently criminalise all forms of discrimination, whether directly intended or indirectly implied? Shouldn't we pull down the scourges of cronyism and nepotism and replace them with systems that put paramount value on efficiency, professionalism, results, creativity, innovation, critical thinking and competence?

Should we not now, once and for all, bury the age-old skeletons of corruption under systems of equitable rewards, closed-loop accountability, penal motivations of the highest order, and inalienable commitment to zero tolerance? Shouldn't we, without fear or favour, end the cycle of divorce that exists between the electorates and the elected and introduce a system that institutionalises communication between the two? Shouldn't we, with grave remorse, replace the dysfunctional economic policy formulations that hinge on the theories of textbooks and advisory strategies of self-seeking wolf-consultants with systems that consistently demand all-inclusiveness, non-discrimination and long-term value sustainability as minimum benchmarks for all our economic and development policy formulations?

Shouldn't we, for the sake of God, posterity and country, break down the foundations of change-resistant institutions and in their place develop institution-wide systems that not only embrace continuous change, but thrive on it for their very existence and success? Shall we not cease to exist as silos, functionally detached from the rest of the world and wallowing in the perpetual delusion that we will catch up with the rest of the world even in our disconnected state? Shouldn't we rather wake up to the reality that if we fail, sooner rather than later, to integrate technology with the main stream of all our economic, political, social and development efforts, we risk not only going back in time whilst the rest of the world moves on, but falling drastically short of the development needed to transform us, our economies and societies from being malnourished prey in the global scheme of evolution?

Maybe then Africa will begin to turn out for the better or maybe not. I do not know. What I do know is that without functional, self-auditing systems to minimize the manipulations that emanate from our inherently fallible and greedy natures, we can only guarantee a never-ending journey where every two steps forward will be followed by five backwards. You be the judge.

Dare I ask more? Yes, maybe I should ask: how, then, shall we chart a better course?

Should our Christian spiritual leaders not inspire their many faithful followers *(the sons and daughters of Africa)*, to recognize that hard work is just as holy as having faith and that one's depth of thinking and intensity of hard work is a reflection of his faith? Should they not remind our people, that ONLY staying on one's knees, hands clasped and eyes closed, is an indictment against the creative power of God in us all and that it ought to be combined with staying on one's feet, to work – hands labouring to turn vision into manifested realities? Does the Holy Book not say that *"the hand of the diligent will rule, but the lazy man will be put to forced labour?"* And does it not also say that *"the rich rule over the poor, and the borrower will always be a servant to the lender?"*

Shall we not put aside, therefore, the fatal doctrine of laziness that says – to ask of God and remain expectant by the folding of arms is the exercise of faith? Instead, shall we not embrace the truth, that faith is walking in the image of God – daring where others won't, because our spirits are limitless beyond time and space; envisioning the unimaginable, because we see through the eyes of an omniscient God; and creating the unthinkable because, like Him, we are gods in the earth? Should this not be the manner in which a religion that moulds us in a major way, operate to reveal God through us in all His glory? Why should the reflection of our continent's wars, starvation, corruption, and failures be the reflection of Africa's God?

Should we not, as a continent and a people, awake from all naivety and gain a more thorough understanding of how the world really works? Should we not understand that every piece of information that gives us an advantage of any sort will never come to us on silver platters because such, in itself, puts others at a disadvantage? Should we not understand that, contrary to cunning diplomatic illusions, every man, people, nation or continent that offers a handshake of help or friendship towards us does so not out of benevolence, but for their own advantage first, not ours? Shouldn't we understand more thoroughly that to be isolated in any way is to set oneself up to be preyed upon, whether in terms of economic policy or diplomacy and that choosing alliances means choosing between all the various shrewd and ruthless devils and not angels?

Shouldn't we understand thoroughly that in the world that Africa is part of, truth is created and never absolute – and whose truth is acceptable depends solely on who can create the most consensuses for theirs? Shall we not understand that modern day survival of nations always requires bargaining, and that every country must have something of value to bargain with, whether it is created, conferred, a threat, or knowledge yet unknown?

Shouldn't we understand this final fundamental truth, that in today's world there are only predators and prey – that the predator reaches the future before everybody else gets there, and the prey always follows; that the predator always creates what everybody else needs and the prey is always the user of such creations, never the creator of it?

Shall we not, then, grasp these truths as being the real manner in which the world works?

And if we did, would it make Africa better?

IO

In Conclusion:
Changing Guards

It is understandable you may be asking the question, *"Why has he only asked the questions and not given the answers?"* That, paradoxically, my brothers and sisters, is exactly the intended answer - that we should all now be questioning ourselves and the world around us, concerning Africa; that the things that we used to casually brush aside because they appeared to be the bigger picture, we would begin to see as our pictures and thus question them; that the things about Africa we used to consider as trivial, not because they impacted us less, but because we had become used to them, will start facing up to our questioning minds; that the so-called truths we used to accept before, by virtue of who told it or how it was told and when or in what circumstances it was told to us, will now be accepted or rejected on the basis of our own known truths, not the purported truths of others.

If you finish reading this book and are in two minds about an assertion you personally held about Africa, it will have served its purpose. If it makes you re-assess what you thought was a settled truth or lie, it will have served its purpose. If it makes you, for the first time ever, question the why, how, when, what, who, which and where of Africa, it will have been to me, a successful book. But even if you didn't ask questions, even if all you did was to take a long pause to assure yourself that the things you believed about Africa are the things you really want to believe about Africa, then this book would still have been fruitful. Above all, if all this book did was to bring you to the conclusion, albeit even philosophically, that some things about Africa have to change, it will be nonetheless, a victory.

My interest is not in the answers you may have to the questions I have asked here, because there will be many of them; nor is my interest in the disagreements or objections you may have to some of the questions and assertions I have raised here and the manner in which I raised them – believe me, I myself have many times questioned my own questions. No, my interest is in sparking in your mind bigger and much more probing questions than these – questions about Africa, your own country, and yourself as an African.

Proverbially, most dogs would feel comfortable if you were to dip their hind limbs into a pond. The same would happen with its forelimbs. If you dipped its entire body, from the neck downwards, into the same pond, it might just get excited enough to swim around a few laps. If, however, you kept its entire body out of the water and immersed only its head, the storyline would change. The dog's entire body will go into frenzy; every muscle and fibre in it will suddenly become viciously alive, fighting everything to get back its breath. At that point, all it needs is air. Replace the dog in the experiment with any terrestrial mammal and the results are likely to be the same. Of course, it is the drowning head, the water-filled nose, the imbalanced eardrums and the sensors of the brain that felt the drowning most, yet the head could do nothing to wrestle itself from the force that held it beneath the water – it had to take the restlessness of the mus-cle-rich body.

You see, the head could be representative of a country or a continent and the rest of the body, its people, over whom the head takes responsibility for coordination, distribution of air and blood, envisioning of the future, sensing of needs, strategizing responses to ailments and the rest. Here is the fascinating obser-vation – whilst the head drowned, the restlessness of the legs alone couldn't have rescued it, nor could the left arm alone. We arrive at the point I needed us to get to: for Africa or its individ-ual nations to *"get out from underneath the water"*, it will require a critical mass or a critical muscle of Africans who can think a certain "positively restless" way together, catch a certain mental and attitudinal revival together or who better still, feel the pain of Africa's suppressed opportunities deeply enough to become rest-less together, and sufficiently restless to counter the distractions of greed, tribal divisions, political partitions and mediocrity.

For now, the *"critical mass"* is building gradually under the still waters of Africa's mundane status quo. And I refuse to believe that mass is a minority, rather, it is a *"small majority"* – and the secret lies in the new generation of Africans, those who are more connected to the rest of the world, those who can see all around them that there is more Africa can be entitled to than it currently gets.

Until we reach that *critical mass*; until we reach that frequency of progressive mental restlessness in our expectations of ourselves, our countries and the continent of Africa, until then, we will still be asking the question – is this why Africa is….?

Author's other works

Title: Diamonds in Eden: How to unearth the treasures hidden in you (E-book & Paperback)

Description: This book shows how a particular success will work for no one else but you alone

Availability: Amazon & Kindle

Title: Doing Business with God (E-book & Paperback)

Description: 60 shocking biblical principles for extraordinary leadership, business and politics.

Availability: Amazon & Kindle

Title: Midnight Philosophies (E-book & Paperback)

Description: My Deep thoughts, Philosophies, Reflections – Whispers of my mind.

Availability: Amazon & Kindle

Title: This Child of Mine (E-book & Paperback)

Description: A refreshing journey on how to "*teach your child in the way s/he should go*"

Availability: Amazon & Kindle

Title: Bible-by-Heart (Mobile App)

Description: A simple but effective App to help anyone memorize up to 500 Bible verses in a year.

Availability: iTunes & Google Play Stores

Title: Holy Rat (Mobile Game)

Description: An exciting Christian mobile game that unwittingly gets you addicted to the word.

Availability: iTunes & Google Play Stores

Title: Godinspiration- "Thus says the Lord" (MP3 Download)

Description: A stimulating voice collection of Bible verses starting with "Thus Says the Lord"

Availability: Amazon MP3

Title: Godinspiration - "The Lord is" (MP3 Download)

Description: A powerful compilation of spoken verses on who the Lord says He is to you.

Availability: Amazon MP3

Title: Godinspiration - "I am, I am" (MP3 Download)

Description: A highly inspirational spoken collection on Bible scriptures about God's "I AM" factor.

Availability: Amazon MP3

Title: The Deputy Minister for Corruption (E-book & Paperback)

Description: A Novel (out in November 2014)

Availability: Amazon & Kindle

Title: A Dove in the Storm (E-book & Paperback)

Description: A Novel (out in November 2014)

Availability: Amazon & Kindle

About the Author

Marricke Kofi Gane is an African author, philosopher, public speaker, a chartered accountant and an educationist. He is married with three children and currently lives in United Kingdom. For more on him, visit www.marrickekofigane.com

www.ingramcontent.com/pod-product-compliance
Lightning Source LLC
Chambersburg PA
CBHW071905020426
42331CB00010B/2679